One Glorious Summer

One Glorious Summer

A PHOTOGRAPHIC HISTORY
OF THE 1996 ATLANTA OLYMPICS

By Glenn Hannigan and Robert Mashburn
AND THE PHOTOGRAPHY STAFF
OF THE ATLANTA JOURNAL AND THE ATLANTA CONSTITUTION
AND COX NEWSPAPERS, DIRECTED BY JOHN GLENN

Text: Glenn Hannigan
Editor: Robert Mashburn
Photo editor: Calvin Cruce
Cover photo: W.A. Bridges Jr.
Cover design: Rhino Graphics

The Atlanta Journal and The Atlanta Constitution
Publisher: Roger S. Kintzel
Editor: Ron Martin
Managing editor: John Walter
Olympics editor: Thomas Oliver
Sports editor: Don Boykin
Photo editor: John Glenn
Graphics and photo director: Tony DeFeria

Published and distributed by Longstreet Press
A subsidiary of Cox Newspapers
A division of Cox Enterprises
2140 Newmarket Parkway
Suite 118
Marietta, Georgia 30067

This book was produced on Macintosh computers
using Quark XPress software.
Film prep and color separations by Hi-Tech Color and Creative Services.

First edition

Manufactured in the United States of America
Printed by R.R. Donnelley & Sons, Willard, Ohio

ISBN:: 1-56352-410-4

CONTENTS

BULGARIA'S JORDAN JOVTCHEV WAS
CAUGHT ON MULTIPLE EXPOSURE,
COMPETING IN THE VAULT.

JOEY IVANSCO

INTRODUCTION

Scenes Great and Small

MUHAMMAD ALI LIGHTING THE CALDRON. MICHAEL Johnson pulling away in the 200. Carl Lewis sailing far and high in the long jump. Kerri Strug snug in the arms of Bela Karolyi.

The enduring images of '96.

Far removed from the marquee players of prime-time events were other poignant moments: the joyous, continuous celebration along the torch-relay route; families laughing and splashing at the Centennial Park fountain; and the large, festive, international throngs of thousands, all over the city.

There were many unforgettable moments in the summer of '96: cheers and tears, triumph and tragedy, joy and crushing defeat, all integral to understanding the scope of the story.

We experienced this incomparable event together, celebrated it together, endured it together. Consider this book an extension of your family vacation photo album. This is your Atlanta family. Your Atlanta experience. You don't even have to trim or mount the pictures.

The Atlanta Journal and Constitution photographers, with the help of 10 colleagues from other Cox newspapers, shot approximately 100,000 frames during the 17 days of the Games. The staff left few stones unturned, even taking the unusual step of purchasing tickets and shooting from grandstand seats when credentials were not available. Many of the 200 photos in this book have not been published previously.

In searching through the newspaper's Olympic files, we didn't always opt for the photo of the day's big story, the big event, or the most recognizable face. Our mission was to accurately reflect the incredible drama, joy, excitement and energy that consumed Atlanta in '96.

Call it One Glorious Summer.

ONE DAY BEFORE OPEN
WAS A CITY AGLOW AS
PREPARED TO PASS THE

g Ceremonies, Atlanta
beaming Ruth Nortje
ame to Shadrack Hoff.

GREG LOVETT

CHAPTER 1

A New Atlanta

IN THE SIX-YEAR GAP BETWEEN THE BID AND THE
START OF THE GAMES, STEEL, CONCRETE AND CRANES
BECAME AS COMMONPLACE AS RED CLAY AND KUDZU.

JOEY IVANSCO

IRON WORKERS BOLTED DOWN TRUSS SUPPORTS FOR ROOF AT GEORGIA TECH'S AQUATIC CENTER, FEBRUARY 1995.

CHARLOTTE B. TEAGLE

1 A NEW ATLANTA

Mad Dash to the Finish Line

THE CACOPHONY OF JACKHAMMERS, BULLDOZERS, DUMP TRUCKS AND SLEDGEHAMMERS echoed without relent, often seven days a week.

With 100 days remaining to the Games, none of the 12 new competition venues was complete. The $235 million Olympic stadium, the heavy lifting done, still required weeks of finishing touches. Progress at the aquatic center was slowed to a crawl by the frightening collapse of a huge steel crossbeam. Centennial Olympic Park was little more than a 21-acre mudpie. At one point, helicopters were called in, in an attempt to dry the ground so work could continue.

NICK ARROYO

Downtown, ripped-up sidewalks and debris from restoration projects littered walkways, making a lunch trip a noisy annoyance, if not a health hazard. Some unassuming office workers literally got stuck in the street, shoes caught in freshly applied tar in the midst of harried, final-minute resurfacing.

All the while, officials of the Atlanta Committee for the Olympic Games voiced full assurance that preparations were "on time and on budget" — not completely convincing to downtown employees, who watched in amazement as crews poured concrete and installed sidewalk tiles in cold and rain.

The task was monumental, with over $1 billion allocated. In addition to the sports venues and the construction of the huge Olympic Village and 21-acre park, roads were repaired, bridges replaced, thousands of shrubs and trees planted and the airport renovated.

Workers sprinted to the finish, hammering nails and applying final coats of paint just hours before Opening Ceremony. They made it.

On July 19, the world welcomed a new Atlanta.

JOEY IVANSCO

ATLANTA'S OLYMPIC DREAMER, BILLY PAYNE, ENVISIONED A FESTIVE GATHERING PLACE DOWNTOWN. OLYMPIC CENTENNIAL PARK, LITTLE MORE THAN TIRE TRACKS ON CLAY IN FEBRUARY 1996, WAS BUILT BETWEEN TECHWOOD DRIVE AND INTERNATIONAL BOULEVARD, A SITE PREVIOUSLY COVERED BY DECAYING BUILDINGS. BY JULY, THE REMARKABLE TRANSFORMATION WAS COMPLETE.

THE 1996 ATLANTA OLYMPICS

WITH CONSTRUCTION OF THE OLYMPIC VILLAGE IN FULL SWING IN JANUARY 1995, ATLANTA'S SKYLINE UNDERWENT DRAMATIC REVISION.

PHIL SKINNER

ONE GLORIOUS SUMMER

DAVID TULIS

IN THE FINAL WEEK OF PREPPING, PETER ACKEN LEARNED THE ROPES AT HOUSE OF BLUES; AT LA MAISON DE L'AFRIQUE, ROGER STEWART HUNG FLAGS OF AFRICAN NATIONS; AND A CONSTRUCTION CREW PAUSED TO CAPTURE THE TORCH RELAY.

GREG LOVETT

JOHN SPINK

THE DAZZLING AQUATIC CENTER AT GEORGIA TECH
WAS STILL A WORK IN PROGRESS WHEN IT HOSTED
WORLD CUP WATER POLO IN SEPTEMBER 1995.

RICH MAHAN

Little more than a javelin toss from Atlanta-Fulton County Stadium, workers toiled for three years, through winter chill, summer heat and year-round mud to complete the signature structure of '96 — the Olympic Stadium.

Photos by JOEY IVANSCO

ONE GLORIOUS SUMMER

THE YEAR BEFORE THE GAMES, THOUGH ORGANIZERS HAD NO
MOUNTAINS TO MOVE, MANY STONES WERE STILL LEFT UNTURNED.
THE TENNIS CENTER (LEFT) WAS LITTLE MORE THAN A SHELL.
AT THE OCOEE RIVER COURSE, ENGINEERS WORKED BOULDER BY
BOULDER TO CONSTRUCT A NATURAL-RIVER, CANOE-KAYAK COURSE.

RICH ADDICKS

JOEY IVANSCO

In the days and weeks leading to the Games, workers pulled long shifts to complete downtown road and sidewalk projects. On Peachtree Street, the Flatiron Building was adorned with a giant medal. At Stone Mountain, 13 months before the Games, the new high-tech velodrome was but a steel skeleton.

ONE GLORIOUS SUMMER

RICH ADDICKS

JOEY IVANSCO

ONE GLORIOUS SUMMER

JEAN SHIFRIN

New lights unto Atlanta: At the Georgia Dome, 16 huge steel derricks, complete with spotlights, grace the 6.5-acre plaza (far left). In Centennial Park, workers toiled high and low to complete the centerpiece of the Games.

RICH ADDICKS

CHAPTER 2

Spectacular Start

EARLY IN THE MORNING, JULY 19, A SPONTANEOUS, BOISTEROUS
STREET CELEBRATION BROKE OUT IN BUCKHEAD AS THOUSANDS
GREETED TORCHBEARERS ON THE FINAL LEG OF THE RELAY.

E.A. KENNEDY III

RICH MAHAN

One Glorious Summer

An Opening to Dazzle the World

SINCE THE MAGIC DAY ATLANTA WAS AWARDED THE GAMES, SEPTEMBER 18, 1990, anticipation grew slowly and steadily, like a distant tidal wave, promising to swamp the city one day.

But when the great surge inevitably arrived, Atlanta's baptism came by fire, not water. The most recognizable fire in the world — the Olympic flame.

For weeks, months, the infamous torch, ignited in Greece by the rays of the sun, coursed its way across Europe, then the U.S., gaining momentum as it worked toward its ultimate destination.

If, until that point, the official countdown seemed to plod along, 1,230 days to go ... 986 days ... 641 ... 417 ... the torch relay made it real, and urgent. No turning back. For the first time, Atlantans could literally see the arrival of the Games, step-by-step, delivered by people great and small in a series of joyful handoffs.

Along the torch route, emotions ran deep, catching many by surprise. Crowds, like moths drawn to flame, waited patiently at all hours of the day and night, cheering wildly, often moved to tears.

Spectators weren't the only ones affected. Torchbearers, even self-professed jaded journalists, described carrying the flame in almost spiritual terms, a reaction few seemed to antici-pate or fully understand.

ALLEN
EYESTONE

The closer the torch drew to Atlanta, the larger, louder, more enthusiastic the crowds became, spilling into the streets, a spontaneous, rolling block party. Before the first pitch was thrown, arrow shot or medal awarded, the tone had already been set. This would be a joyous, 17-day, open-armed celebration.

As the Opening Ceremony dazzled spectators and viewers with its brilliant choreography and stunning visual displays, the flame traveled the final miles of its journey through the streets of downtown. Atlanta was off to a remarkable start. All that remained to officially set the Games in motion was the climactic lighting of the caldron.

And they saved The Greatest for last.

THE CENTENNIAL GAMES KICKED OFF
WITH A DAZZLING OPENING PAGEANT,
FEATURING HUNDREDS
OF PERFORMERS YOUNG AND OLD,
CELEBRATING CUSTOMS AND
CULTURES FROM AROUND THE WORLD.

ONE GLORIOUS SUMMER

ALLEN EYESTONE

RICH ADDICKS

JOEY IVANSCO

ONE GLORIOUS SUMMER

WRESTLER BRUCE BAUMGARTNER WAS GIVEN THE HONOR OF CARRYING THE COLORS FOR TEAM USA DURING THE PARADE OF NATIONS. A RECORD 10,700 ATHLETES, MOSTLY WAVING AND SMILING TO THE CHEERING CROWD, FILLED THE OLYMPIC STADIUM INFIELD.

JONATHAN NEWTON

SURROUNDED BY ATHLETES FROM 197 NATIONS, ACOG CHIEF BILLY PAYNE AND IOC CHAIRMAN JUAN ANTONIO SAMARANCH DELIVERED OPENING REMARKS. PRESIDENT BILL CLINTON RECEIVED A MEMENTO FROM USOC PRESIDENT LEROY WALKER. THE CALDRON WAS AGLOW, SIGNIFYING THE OFFICIAL START OF GAMES.

ONE GLORIOUS SUMMER

CHAPTER 3

Magic Moments

CARL LEWIS DEFIED BOTH GRAVITY AND THE NATURAL
AGING PROCESS, SOARING TO VICTORY IN THE LONG JUMP.

RICH ADDICKS

E.A. KENNEDY III

3 MAGIC MOMENTS

Enduring Images of Triumph

THE CROWD IS FOCUSED, KEENLY AWARE SOMETHING EXTRAORDINARY MAY BE CLOSE AT hand. The difference between legend and also-ran is often measured in tiny fractions of seconds, indistinguishable to the naked eye.

When the best athletes in the world square off, focused for years on one single moment, tension is thick, the stakes great. For some spectators, lucky enough to view a historic showdown, it's a chance to gloat, "I was there the night ..."

All the planning, money, great weather and grand architecture in the world can't make an Olympics spectacular. What makes it special are the rare moments that transcend sport. Dramatic upsets. Heroic struggles. Superhuman achievements.

Atlanta was blessed with more than its share in '96, including various world records and remarkable individual performances.

Who was most memorable? Kerri Strug, Michael Johnson (right), Carl Lewis, Amy Van Dyken, Naim Suleymanoglu (left), Donovan Bailey, Dan O'Brien, or any number of others?

Depends on your vantage point. Blink, and you could miss history.

JONATHAN NEWTON

Michael Johnson, who entered the Games as the marquee attraction, was overshadowed his first big night, having the misfortune of winning the 400 meters the same evening Carl Lewis pulled off a stunning victory in the long jump. A thrilling, magic moment.

Days later, Johnson returned to complete an unprecedented double by winning the 200 meters, shattering the world record. Johnson's expression as he ran past the finish line is one people will not soon forget.

Unless you missed it.

Just in case, it's included here.

DAVID TULIS

JONATHAN NEWTON

U.S. SPRINTER GAIL DEVERS,
THE DEFENDING 100-METER
CHAMPION FROM BARCELONA,
JOYFULLY LEAPED INTO THE
ARMS OF COACH BOBBY KERSEE
AFTER HER STUNNING ENCORE
IN ATLANTA. DEVERS WON THE
WOMEN'S PREMIER TRACK EVENT
IN A PHOTO FINISH.

ONE GLORIOUS SUMMER

RICH ADDICKS

CANADA'S DONOVAN BAILEY PULLED AWAY IN THE MEN'S 100-METER DASH, LEAVING NAMIBIA'S FRANK FREDERICKS AND TRINIDAD'S ATO BOLDON TO FIGHT FOR SILVER, WHICH WENT TO FREDERICKS.

RICH ADDICKS

ONE GLORIOUS SUMMER

FRANK NIEMEIR

HE'S SIMPLY THE BEST ... OF ALL TIME. DONOVAN BAILEY MADE
A FORCEFUL CLAIM TO TITLE OF WORLD'S FASTEST MAN,
EXALTING IN HIS 100-METER VICTORY IN A WORLD-RECORD
PERFORMANCE OF 9.84 SECONDS.

JOEY IVANSCO

ONE GLORIOUS SUMMER

RICH ADDICKS

DAN O'BRIEN, WHOSE POLE VAULT MISHAP AT THE 1992 OLYMPIC TRIALS DENIED
HIM A SPOT ON THE U.S. TEAM, COULD NOT BE DENIED IN '96. HE WON THE
DECATHLON TO STAKE HIS CLAIM TO THE TITLE OF WORLD'S GREATEST ATHLETE.

ONE MAN STOOD ALONE. MICHAEL JOHNSON OF THE U.S., WHO HAD ALREADY WON THE 400 METERS, COMPLETED AN UNPRECEDENTED DOUBLE-GOLD PERFORMANCE WITH A DOMINATING WORLD-RECORD VICTORY IN THE 200.

JONATHAN NEWTON

A WOMEN'S TOUCH: ITALY'S GIOVANNA TRILLINI (ABOVE) AND GERMANY'S
ANJA FICHTEL MAURITZ (RIGHT) REJOICED AFTER SCORING EFFECTIVE
"TOUCHES" IN THEIR RESPECTIVE MATCHES. TRILLINI HELPED ITALY WIN GOLD
IN THE TEAM FOIL, MAURITZ AND HER TEAMMATES EARNED BRONZE.

PYRROS DIMAS OF GREECE
WHO SAID HE "CAME HERE
TO WIN THE GOLD," DID
EXACTLY THAT, SETTING
THREE WORLD RECORDS
EN ROUTE TO CAPTURING
THE 183-POUND
WEIGHTLIFTING CLASS.
GERMANY'S MARC HUSTER
(FAR RIGHT)
FINISHED SECOND.

DAVID TULIS

DAVID TULIS

NOT ALL THAT GLOWS IS GOLD: AMERICAN TIM MCRAE,
WHO FINISHED OUT OF THE MEDALS RACE IN THE
154-POUND CLASS, HAD PLENTY TO CELEBRATE — A U.S.
RECORD OF 177.5 KILOGRAMS IN THE CLEAN AND JERK.

POWER AND GRACE: JOHN ROETHLISBERGER OF THE U.S. (FAR RIGHT) APPEARED TO REACH LOW ORBIT DURING VAULT COMPETITION. GERMANY'S STRONG-ARMED ANDREAS WECKER MUSCLED HIS WAY TO GOLD IN THE HORIZONTAL BAR EVENT.

JOHN SPINK

JOHN SPINK

RENEE HANNANS

U.S. BOXER DAVID REID, AN UNDERDOG BEING OUTFOUGHT BY CUBA'S ALFREDO DUVERGEL IN THE 156-POUND CHAMPIONSHIP BOUT, STUNNED THE CROWD, AND HIS OPPONENT, WITH A DRAMATIC, LATE KNOCKOUT TO GIVE THE HOME TEAM ITS ONLY GOLD MEDAL IN BOXING.

WILLIAM BERRY

CHINA'S FU MINGXIA, WHO WON THE SPRINGBOARD AND PLATFORM DIVING,
BECAME THE FIRST WOMAN TO WIN THE DOUBLE GOLD SINCE 1960.

ONE GLORIOUS SUMMER

THE OFFICIAL CENTENNIAL GAMES logo made a dramatic backdrop for springboard diver MICHAEL KUEHNE of GERMANY.

RICH ADDICKS

SKIP PETERSON

ONE GLORIOUS SUMMER

THE SALUTE OF CHAMPIONS: ATTILA CZENE OF HUNGARY (LEFT) REACTS TO HIS VICTORY IN THE 200 INDIVIDUAL MEDLEY. AMY VAN DYKEN ENJOYED THE SWEET TASTE OF VICTORY FOUR TIMES, THE MOST GOLD EVER WON BY AN AMERICAN WOMAN IN AN OLYMPIAD.

SKIP PETERSON

WILLIAM BERRY

IT'S ONWARD AND UPWARD FOR U.S. SWIMMER TOM DOLAN, WHO OVERCAME A SMALL DEFICIT IN THE FINAL 50 METERS OF THE 400-METER INDIVIDUAL MEDLEY TO TAKE THE GOLD.

ONE GLORIOUS SUMMER

THE EXPRESSION ON JORDI SANS' FACE MADE IT CLEAR: VICTORY FOR SPAIN,
WHICH KNOCKED OFF CROATIA IN THE CHAMPIONSHIP GAME OF WATER POLO.

WILLIAM BERRY

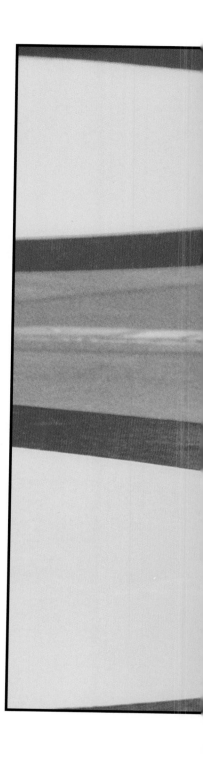

WILLIAM BERRY

AMERICAN KURT ANGLE, WHOSE FIERCE STRUGGLE WITH IRAN'S ABBAS JADIDI IN THE
220-POUND DIVISION OF FREESTYLE WRESTLING ENDED IN A DRAW, IS OVERCOME BY
EMOTION AFTER BEING AWARDED THE JUDGES' DECISION — AND THE GOLD.

THE 1996 ATLANTA OLYMPICS

JONATHAN NEWTON

THE THRILL OF IT ALL: BRANDON PAULSON OF THE U.S. (RIGHT)
CELEBRATED A SEMIFINAL VICTORY IN 114-POUND GRECO-
ROMAN WRESTLING. SOUTH KOREA'S SIM KWON-HO (ABOVE)
BESTED ALEXANDER PAVLOV IN THE 105-POUND CLASS.

IN MEN'S VOLLEYBALL, NETHERLANDS KNOCKED OFF ITALY FOR GOLD.
IN WOMEN'S JUDO, CUBA'S DRIULIS GONZALEZ SLAMMED SOUTH
KOREA'S JUNG SUN-YONG TO CAPTURE THE LIGHTWEIGHT DIVISION.

ONE GLORIOUS SUMMER

GREG LOVETT

CUBA'S BASEBALL TEAM PROVED ONCE AGAIN BEST IN THE WORLD, WHILE A DISAPPOINTED U.S. FINISHED WITH THE BRONZE. THE DREAM TEAM, INCLUDING SHAQ O'NEAL AND KARL MALONE, EASILY WON AGAIN. IN PERHAPS THE BIGGEST SURPRISE OF THE GAMES, NIGERIA DEFEATED POWERFUL ARGENTINA IN THE MEN'S SOCCER FINAL.

THE MAN IN THE MIDDLE,
ALLEN JOHNSON OF THE
U.S., HELD HIS GROUND
AND WON THE 110
HURDLES IN RECORD
OLYMPIC TIME.

JONATHAN NEWTON

ONE MORE TIME: 35-YEAR-OLD CARL LEWIS THRILLED THE CROWD WITH A FOURTH STRAIGHT GOLD IN THE LONG JUMP, GIVING HIM AN OLYMPIC RECORD-TYING NINE GOLD MEDALS IN A STUNNING CAREER.

RICH ADDICKS

LOUIE FAVORITE

ONE GLORIOUS SUMMER

JONATHAN NEWTON

JOHN SPINK

FLYING THE COLORS: FATUMA ROBA OF ETHIOPIA (LEFT AND FAR LEFT) WAS THE WOMEN'S MARATHON CHAMPION; CATHY FREEMAN OF AUSTRALIA (ABOVE) FINISHED SECOND IN THE 400 METER TO MARIE-JOSE PEREC OF FRANCE (BELOW), WHO ALSO WON THE 200.

RENEE HANNANS

A STUNNING COURSE OF EVENTS: NORWAY'S VEBJOERN RADAL APPEARED SHOCKED BY HIS UPSET VICTORY IN THE MEN'S 800. BY THE LOOK OF SOME OF HIS COMPETITORS, HE WASN'T ALONE.

MARLENE KARAS

CHAPTER 4

LIKE MANY VENUES, THE OLYMPIC STADIUM WAS
A DIFFICULT PLACE TO FIND AN EMPTY SEAT.

A World Gathering

W.A. BRIDGES JR.

ONE GLORIOUS SUMMER

A Crowd for Every Occasion

FOR 17 DAYS, IT WAS PART CARNIVAL, PART STREET FESTIVAL.

Atlanta invited the world to its coming-out party and, by the looks of the packed venues and overflowing sidewalks, few sent regrets. Throughout downtown, though car traffic was surprisingly light, the streets were energized with a vibrant international pulse and flavor.

For Atlanta veterans, accustomed to closed shops and empty parking lots by dusk, the impact was profound and surreal.

Atlanta. An Olympic city. Unbelievable.

Though some IOC potentates groused about too many vendors, the vendors griped about too few customers, and the international press complained about too much, period, the sidewalk-crushing crowds had a different spin on the Centennial Games. They were sensational.

Certainly, L.A. made more money and historic Barcelona provided a more picturesque backdrop, but neither could match Atlanta at the places it matters most — the spirit and attitude of the people.

From polite workers, helpful volunteers and excited spectators to patient MARTA riders and determined pin traders, the people set the tone: laughing, smiling, helping, cheering and dancing.

DAVID TULIS

Spectators from the nations of the world proudly displayed flags where it was hard to ignore them — on their faces. Children of all ages were included, moms and dads pushing strollers through downtown into the wee hours of the morning.

Never before have crowds like this packed Olympics events. The 8.5 million tickets sold were more than L.A. and Barcelona combined. Signs and scalpers were everywhere — Tickets Wanted! — at every event from archery to wrestling.

These were the largest Games ever. The fastest ever. The most-watched ever. And, in the hearts of many, the greatest ever.

NO OPEN SPACE WAS SAFE.
IF PINHEADS RAN OUT OF
ROOM ON THEIR HATS,
ALMOST ANY ARTICLE OF
CLOTHING WOULD DO
JUST AS NICELY.

KAREN WARREN

DAVID TULIS

ONE GLORIOUS SUMMER

RICH MAHAN

RICH MAHAN

THE UNOFFICIAL CURRENCY OF
THE OLYMPIC GAMES — LITTLE
METAL PINS — COULD BE
FOUND VIRTUALLY EVERYWHERE:
AT VENUES, ON THE STREETS,
ON VOLUNTEERS, WORKERS,
AND EVEN ON MANY ATHLETES.

ENTRANCE ENTRANCE

W.A. BRIDGES JR.

JEAN SHIFRIN

ONE GLORIOUS SUMMER

SCENE ON THE STREETS: AN AIR NATIONAL GUARDSMAN, ON CROWD CONTROL, STOPPED FOR A CHAT WITH VENDOR DIANE HURLEY, SELLING "BODY TEASE" SHIRTS. VENUE VOLUNTEER JOHN LAMOREAUX EXAMINED A THERMOMETER, WHICH APPEARED CLOSE TO MAXING OUT. AND VENDOR ANTONIO LOCKETT DISCUSSED THE PRICE OF UNPRECIOUS MEDAL WITH JONI MOORE OF WARNER ROBBINS.

WILLIAM BERRY

SCOTT MARTIN

JOHN SPINK

IT'S ONE THING TO WEAR YOUR HEART ON YOUR SLEEVE,
AND ANOTHER TO WEAR YOUR FLAG ON YOUR FACE.
JAY WALSH OF BOSTON DIDN'T NEED TO WAVE OLD GLORY AT
THE MEN'S ROAD CYCLING EVENT TO REVEAL HIS TRUE COLORS.

RICH MAHAN

ENTHUSIASM WAS CONTAGIOUS: FLAG-WAVING AT OCOEE WHITEWATER
COMPETITION, ARM-WAVING AT BUCKHEAD ROAD CYCLING,
AND HAND-CLAPPING AT ATLANTA BEACH VOLLEYBALL, WHERE
CHELSEA CLINTON (FAR RIGHT) LED CHEERS FOR THE HOME TEAM.

ONE GLORIOUS SUMMER

RICH ADDICKS

WILLIAM BERRY

WILLIAM BERRY

KAREN WARREN

AT THE WORLD CONGRESS CENTER, THE RISING SUN WAS VISIBLE AT EVERY TURN AS JAPANESE FANS LOADED UP WITH BANNERS, HATS AND INNUMERABLE FLAGS TO CHEER THEIR JUDO TEAM.

KAREN WARREN

"ΠΥΡΡΟ ΓΕΡΑ!!! Η ΚΕΡΚΥΡΑ... ΚΟΝΤΑ!"

DAVID TULIS

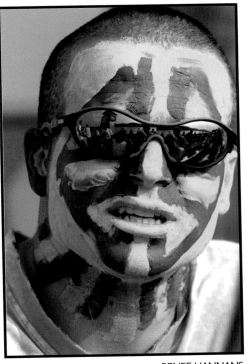

GREEK FANS SHOWED THEIR COLORS — AND ENTHUSIASM — AT THE WEIGHTLIFTING COMPETITION (FAR LEFT). AUSTRALIA'S MATTHEW COLYUHOUN MADE IT EASY FOR COUNTRYMEN TO PICK HIM OUT AT THE KAYAK COMPETITION, AS DID URUGUAY CYCLING FANS JAVIER ALVARES AND JOHNNY MAYERO.

RENEE HANNANS

PHIL SKINNER

FRANK NIEMEIR

THE STARS COME TO TOWN: ACTOR JOHN GOODMAN,
SIGNING SHORTS WORN BY CARESSA AYRES
AT THE HOUSE OF BLUES, MADE AN APPEARANCE ON
HIS HARLEY DAVIDSON. AT THE STONE MOUNTAIN
TENNIS VENUE, BROOKE SHIELDS WAS PRESENT TO
CONGRATULATE ANDRE AGASSI ON HIS GOLD MEDAL.

SKIP PETERSON

ONE GLORIOUS SUMMER

RICH ADDICKS

TECH'S STUNNING NEW AQUATIC CENTER WAS SOLD
OUT FOR VIRTUALLY EVERY EVENT: SWIMMING, DIVING
AND WATER POLO. AT LEFT, ITALIAN WATER POLO FANS
CHEERED TEAM TO BRONZE MEDAL.

THE COOLEST HOT SPOT IN TOWN: FROM THE DAY IT OPENED, THE FOUNTAIN AT CENTENNIAL OLYMPIC PARK WAS A SMASHING SUCCESS.

JEAN SHIFRIN

KAREN WARREN

ONE GLORIOUS SUMMER

ERIC WILLIAMS

PHIL SKINNER

THE BEST VIEW IN TOWN:
NOT ONLY DID CHILDREN
DISCOVER WHAT A GREAT VIEW
YOU GET FROM A STRONG SET
OF SHOULDERS, BUT IT ALSO
OFFERED THE PERFECT
OPPORTUNITY TO SNAG
SUNGLASSES AND PULL HAIR.

RICH ADDICKS

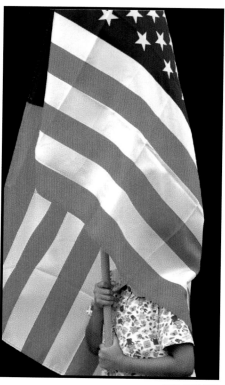

BILL REINKE

A PATRIOTIC THEME: VICTOR SMITH, 2, POSED AS A STAR-SPANGLED IZZY. KRISTEN HUGHES, 7, WRAPPED HERSELF IN OLD GLORY. SEVEN-YEAR OLD KELLY DICKERSON (RIGHT) TRAVELED ALL THE WAY FROM SPARKS, NEVADA, TO ATTEND THE OLYMPICS AND MAY HAVE WON A MEDAL FOR MOST-PATRIOTIC — BUT WORST-FITTING — HAT.

CURTIS COMPTON

THE 1996 ATLANTA OLYMPICS

105

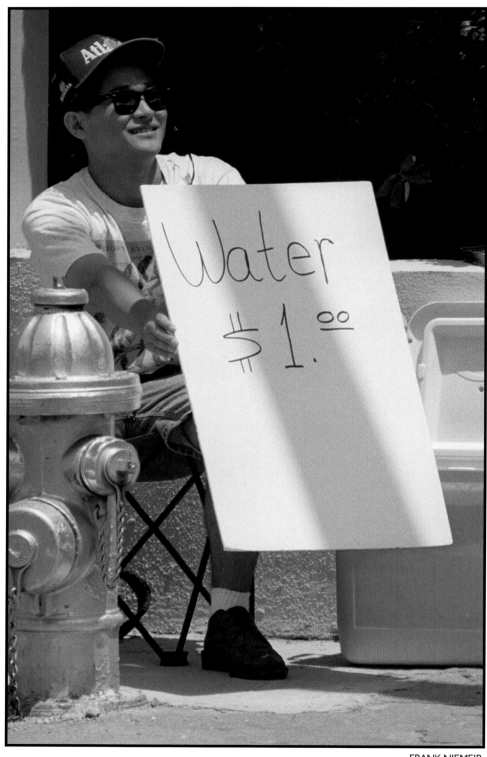

FRANK NIEMEIR

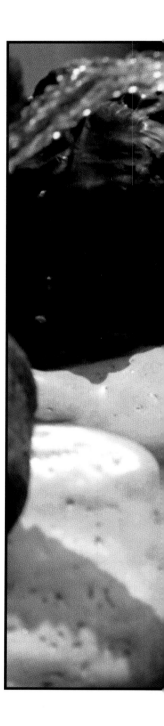

FRANK NIEMEIR

WHILE DOHYUN YOO'S LOW-FRILLS SIDEWALK SHOP CONSISTED OF ONE FOLDING CHAIR, ONE COOLER AND A HAND-DRAWN SIGN, ANNE LOTT OF LANSING, MICHIGAN, FOUND AN EVEN CHEAPER SOURCE OF REFRESHMENT — A WATER-SPEWING SCULPTURE ON INTERNATIONAL BOULEVARD

CHAPTER 5

The Women of '96

DRAPE AN AMERICAN FLAG
ON THE VICTORY STAND
AND FIRE UP THE
"STAR SPANGLED BANNER."
IT WAS A BANNER YEAR FOR
U.S. WOMEN'S TEAMS IN A
VARIETY OF SPORTS AND
VENUES, FROM ATHENS TO
ATLANTA TO COLUMBUS.

DAVID TULIS

5 THE WOMEN OF '96

U.S. Vaults into Spotlight

IT WAS EXPECTED TO BE THE OLYMPIC "YEAR OF THE WOMAN." AND, IN MANY WAYS, IT was a promise fulfilled. Except someone, somewhere, should have penciled in the letters "U.S."

U.S. women dominated the Games like a weekend intramural meet. They won gold in Atlanta, Athens and Columbus; on the track, the court, the pool, the gym, the pitch and diamond.

While '96 marked a substantial increase in the inclusion and participation of women, the U.S. made certain there was also a marked increase in thrills, as well.

Could a movie-of-the-week have been more compelling than the real-life drama at the gymnastics final? In the defining moment of the Games, Kerri Strug, who just minutes before had seriously injured her left ankle on a botched landing, needed to successfully complete a final vault to give the U.S. its first team victory ever. Her heroic effort ranks as one of the most courageous Olympic moments ever.

U.S. women, as expected, dominated basketball and tennis. In track and swimming, they won every relay event, with swimmer Amy Van Dyken winning a record four gold medals.

In new events, it was U.S. women winning the gold in softball and soccer. In synchronized swimming, a team competition for the first time, the U.S. earned a perfect score on the way to the gold.

ALLEN EYESTONE

THE 1996 ATLANTA OLYMPICS

THE U.S. 4×100
RELAY TEAM, WITH
ATLANTA'S GWEN
TORRENCE
RUNNING A
BLISTERING
ANCHOR LEG
(PREVIOUS PAGE),
FLEXED ITS
MUSCLES AND RAN
OFF WITH GOLD.

ONE GLORIOUS SUMMER

IN ONE OF THE GAMES' MOST HEROIC EFFORTS, U.S. VETERAN JACKIE JOYNER-KERSEE IGNORED A PAINFUL THIGH INJURY TO WIN BRONZE IN THE LONG JUMP.

KAREN WARREN

DAVID TULIS

In a sport that demands great artistry as well as athleticism, the U.S. showed why it is the premier team in the world, earning perfect marks en route to synchronized swimming gold.

ONE GLORIOUS SUMMER

RICH ADDICKS

THE FRENCH TEAM WAS A PICTURE OF CONCENTRATION SECONDS BEFORE ENTERING THE POOL.

RICH ADDICKS

THE CUBAN VOLLEYBALL
TEAM HAD MUCH TO
CELEBRATE: AN EARLY
VICTORY OVER THE U.S. AND
AN EVENTUAL GOLD MEDAL.

JONATHAN NEWTON

WILLIAM BERRY

ONE GLORIOUS SUMMER

IN A RARE DISAPPOINTMENT FOR U.S. WOMEN,
THE HIGH PROFILE BEACH VOLLEYBALL TANDEM OF HOLLY
MCPEAK (LEFT) AND NANCY RENO (SIGNALING A PLAY),
MADE AN EARLY EXIT AND FINISHED SANS MEDAL.

LILIA PODKOPAYEVA OF THE UKRAINE FLOORED HER
COMPETITION, WINNING TWO INDIVIDUAL GOLDS,
INCLUDING THE WOMEN'S ALL-AROUND TITLE,
AND ADDING A SILVER ON THE BALANCE BEAM.

JOEY IVANSCO

RICH ADDICKS

KERRI STRUG, WHO SERIOUSLY INJURED HER LEFT
ANKLE AFTER A FAULTY VAULT DROPPED HER TO
HER KNEES ON HER FIRST ATTEMPT, NEEDED A GREAT
LEAP OF FAITH, AND NO LACK OF COURAGE,
TO MAKE A FINAL JUMP.

MARLENE KARAS

ONE GLORIOUS SUMMER

STRUG ENDURED SEVERE PAIN, LANDING ON THE PAINFUL ANKLE, BUT REMAINED UPRIGHT LONG ENOUGH TO EARN THE JUDGES' APPROVAL. SHE HAD TO BE HELPED OFF THE FLOOR AND CARRIED TO THE AWARDS PLATFORM.

DAVID TULIS

U.S. GYMNAST SHANNON MILLER WAS THE '96 QUEEN OF THE BEAM. SHE CAPPED A STUNNING CAREER, WHICH INCLUDED A U.S. RECORD SEVEN MEDALS IN TWO OLYMPICS, WITH A GOLD MEDAL ON THE 4-INCH-WIDE APPARATUS.

JOEY IVANSCO

DAVID CRUZ

RICH ADDICKS

DOMINIQUE MOCEANU'S PERFORMANCE ON THE BALANCE BEAM
HELPED THE U.S. TEAM MAKE IT TO THE GOLD MEDAL STAND.

SKIP PETERSON

JOEY IVANSCO

THE U.S. FIELD HOCKEY TEAM, THOUGH NOT A SERIOUS MEDAL CONTENDER,
ENJOYED ITS SHARE OF THRILLS, INCLUDING A SHOCKING LAST-MINUTE UPSET
OF SOUTH KOREA. LELIE LYNESS (ABOVE, LEFT) GREETED BARB MAROIS WITH
OPEN ARMS AFTER MAROIS SCORED THE DRAMATIC WINNING GOAL.

ALLEN EYESTONE

ONE GLORIOUS SUMMER

U.S. PITCHER LISA FERNANDEZ (LEFT) WAS ONE PITCH FROM A PERFECT GAME WHEN SHE YIELDED A TWO-OUT HOME RUN IN THE 10TH INNING AGAINST AUSTRALIA. FERNANDEZ AND MICHELLE GRANGER (ABOVE), LED THE U.S. WOMEN TO THE FIRST FAST-PITCH SOFTBALL GOLD MEDAL.

THE 1996 ATLANTA OLYMPICS

CHINESE TAIPEI
CATCHER HUI-CHUN
YANG WASN'T ABLE
TO HANDLE THE
THROW AS MICHELLE
SMITH OF THE U.S.
SAFELY REACHED
HOME FOR A
SECOND-INNING RUN.

MARLENE KARAS

DAVID TULIS

IT WAS ALL SMILES FOR NIKKI MCRAY (ABOVE) AND
THE U.S. WOMEN'S BASKETBALL TEAM, WHICH
RECOVERED FROM AN UPSET LOSS IN BARCELONA TO
RETURN TO THE GOLD-MEDAL STAND IN ATLANTA.

THE 1996 ATLANTA OLYMPICS

ONE GLORIOUS SUMMER

BARELY OUT OF JUNIOR HIGH SCHOOL, 14-YEAR-OLD AMANDA BEARD OF THE U.S. WON A GOLD MEDAL IN THE 400 MEDLEY RELAY AND BARELY MISSED TWO OTHERS, TAKING SILVER IN THE 100 AND 200 BREASTSTROKES.

ALLEN EYESTONE

IRELAND'S MICHELLE SMITH WAS HANDS ABOVE HER COMPETITION, WINNING THREE INDIVIDUAL GOLDS AND A BRONZE. COSTA RICA'S CLAUDIA POLL CELEBRATED HER VICTORY IN THE 200 FREESTYLE WITH A SALUTE TO HER NATION.

JONATHAN NEWTON

FRANK NIEMEIR

JONATHAN NEWTON

THE U.S. WOMEN'S RELAY TEAMS WERE UNBEATABLE, INCLUDING THE 4×100 FREESTYLE COMBINATION (ABOVE) OF ANGEL MARTINO, CATHERINE FOX, AMY VAN DYKEN AND JENNY THOMPSON.

FRANK NIEMEIR

CHAPTER 6

Heartbreakers

AFTER YEARS OF PREPARATION AND TRAINING, MANY ATHLETES FOUND
ONLY DISAPPOINTMENT AT THE GAMES. U.S. SPRINTER JON DRUMMOND
COVERED HIS HEAD WITH THE FLAG AFTER THE FAVORED 4×100 RELAY
TEAM WAS DEFEATED BY THE CANADIANS.

RICH ADDICKS

The Many Faces of Despair

T HE SMALLEST IMPERFECTION, TINIEST MISCALCULATION, SLIGHTEST SLIP — AND THE opportunity of a lifetime can disappear.

It's a nightmare-come-true many athletes will replay the rest of their lives — the untimely bad break. For every ecstatic gold medalist, flag-waving victor, conquering hero, there's an equally emotional counterbalance, the devastated also-ran.

MARLENE KARAS

Not many Olympians make it to the cover of a Wheaties box, or couch of the "Tonight Show." But often it's the miniscule margin of failure that many find so painful. At the finish of the women's 100 meter, one of the premier events of the Games, competitors were left hanging for minutes while officials studied a photo of the finish. It was Gail Devers by an eyelash.

The reasons for disappointment, apart from superior opposition, are virtually limitless: an untimely injury, equipment problem, illness, adverse weather conditions, poor judges' decision or even a missed bus stop. Of course, it might just be an off day. Even the best gymnast in the world can be foiled by one tiny misstep, a toe on the line, that can make the difference between gold — or no medal at all.

Who can understand the disappointment? Who can empathize? Few, other than world class athletes, will ever know the level of commitment, years of training, dieting and other sacrifices made in the quest for victory.

Or how devastating one little slip can feel.

JOHN SPINK

ONE GLORIOUS SUMMER

Photos by CURTIS COMPTON

WHEN YOUR TEAMMATE IS A HORSE, ANY FALSE STEP
CAN HOLD HARROWING CONSEQUENCES, AS
FRANKE SLOOTHAAK OF GERMANY DISCOVERED.

IN ONE OF THE CLOSEST FINISHES IN MODERN PENTATHLON HISTORY, EDUARD ZENOVKA OF RUSSIA STUMBLED IN THE FINAL EVENT AND FINISHED SECOND TO ALEKSANDR PARYGIN OF KAZAKHSTAN.

ALLEN EYESTONE

ONE GLORIOUS SUMMER

Photos by KAREN WARREN

SO NEAR, YET ... FRANCE'S ERIC BONNEL SMOOTHLY CLEANED 140 KILOGRAMS,
BUT WAS UNABLE TO COMPLETE THE LIFT TO SECOND POSITION, OVER HIS HEAD.

U.S. LONG JUMPER MIKE POWELL, THE WORLD
RECORD HOLDER AND PRE-OLYMPIC FAVORITE, CAME
UP SHORT IN ATLANTA, FAILING TO WIN A MEDAL.

RICH ADDICKS

155

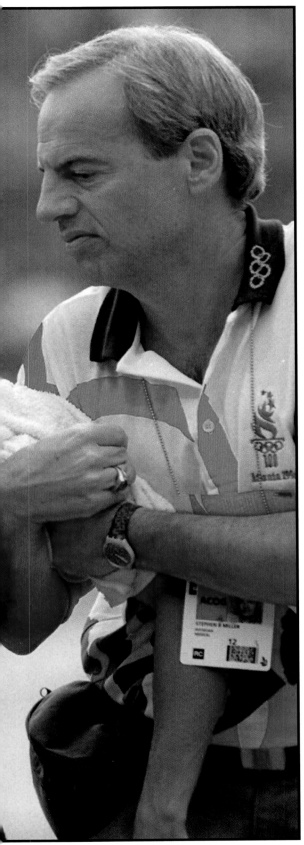

RICH ADDICKS

JOHN SPINK

THE EVENT IS BRUTAL, 26.2 MILES THROUGH THE HOT, HUMID STREETS OF ATLANTA. AFTER SUCCESSFULLY COMPLETING THEIR RUNS ON DIFFERENT DAYS, RITHYA TO OF CAMBODIA AND ANNE MARIE LAUCK OF THE U.S. NEEDED THE ARMS OF OLYMPIC VOLUNTEERS TO CARRY THEM WHEN THEIR LEGS NO LONGER COULD.

It wasn't smooth sailing for Elena Kurzina of Belarus, who faltered in the challenging "Humongos" leg of the Ocoee kayak course, or for Poland's Grzegorz Kaleta and teammate Piotr Markiewicz (next page), who failed to medal in men's flatwater kayak at Lake Lanier.

KAREN WARREN

WHETHER ON THE TRACK AT STONE MOUNTAIN, OR
ON THE ROAD COURSE THROUGH ATLANTA'S STREETS,
THE WORST FATE A CYCLIST COULD ENDURE WAS TO
LOSE HIS WHEELS AND BEND THEM IN THE PROCESS.

RHOSHII WELLS OF RIVERDALE, GA., COULDN'T HIDE HIS DISAPPOINTMENT AFTER LOSING A SEMIFINAL BOUT TO CUBA'S ARIEL HERNANDEZ IN THE 165-POUND DIVISION. WELLS SETTLED FOR A BRONZE MEDAL; HERNANDEZ EARNED GOLD.

ALLEN EYESTONE

CHAPTER 7

Tragedy & Triumph

A HORRIFIC BLAST AT THE HEART AND SOUL OF
THE GAMES, CENTENNIAL OLYMPIC PARK,
THREATENED TO CRUSH THE SPIRIT OF '96. BUT
THE PEOPLE HAD ANOTHER LEGACY IN MIND.

GARY KIRKSEY

DAVID CRUZ

ONE GLORIOUS SUMMER

TRAGEDY & TRIUMPH

"We will not be defeated"

T HE GROUND HAD BARELY STOPPED SMOLDERING AT CENTENNIAL OLYMPIC PARK BEFORE pundits weighed in: The '96 Games would forever be remembered for terrorism, Atlanta as another Munich.

They were wrong. Instant history rarely rings true.

In the summer of '96, though terror stole one night and two lives, it was the people who won back the day, and the spirit of the Games.

What happened July 27, early Saturday morning, was almost unthinkable. An explosion, a terrorist's deadly pipe bomb, ripped through a crowd gathered for a concert, killing two and injuring more than 100.

GREG LOVETT

The shocking act threatened to cast a permanent pall over the Games. Would people return to the park? Would they feel safe in the venues? Would Atlanta be remembered for terror and death?

It didn't take long for people to vote, with their hearts — and feet.

The day after the blast, spectators, though noticeably sullen and restrained, filled venues, the stadium flags at half mast. Sprinkled throughout the crowds were banners of support and signs of determination, "The Games Will Go On."

And so they did.

Three days after the explosion, tens of thousands jammed the park for an emotional memorial service, to pray, pay respects and to reclaim their gathering place. Tears and passion were mixed with a touch of defiance. "This is our Olympics," said one visitor. "We are determined and we will not be defeated."

It was an attitude that grew the remainder of the Games, friends and family drawn closer through tragedy. If anything, the incredibly popular park was more crowded after the bombing than before. And, perhaps, this may be Atlanta's greatest legacy, the proudest moment, the biggest victory.

The spirit of the Games. The people.

With apologies to Michael Johnson and Kerri Strug, may it be remembered so.

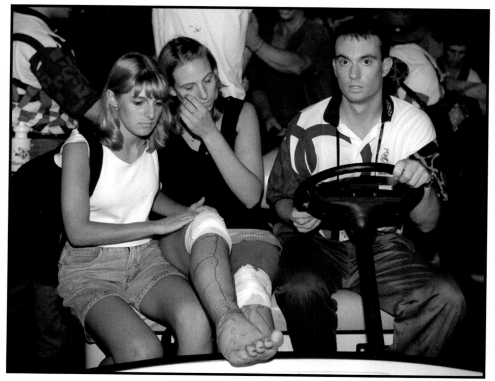

IN THE BOMB'S
AFTERMATH:
VOLUNTEERS SCRAMBLED
TO AID VICTIMS WHILE
AREAS SURROUNDING
THE PARK, MOMENTS
BEFORE OVERFLOWING
WITH PEOPLE, WERE
QUICKLY ABANDONED.

KIRTHMON DOZIER

LAUREL NOEL

ONE GLORIOUS SUMMER

FLOWERS WERE SCATTERED AND A SMALL AMERICAN FLAG WAS PLANTED NEAR THE BASE OF THE CENTENNIAL PARK LIGHT TOWER WHERE THE BOMB EXPLODED, CLAIMING TWO LIVES.

DAVID CRUZ

THE 1996 ATLANTA OLYMPICS

169

OBAL OLYMPIC VILLAGE

CENTENNIAL
OLYMPIC

INVESTIGATORS FROM
VARIOUS AGENCIES
COMBED THE BOMB
SITE, EVEN SEARCHING
ON HANDS AND
KNEES AMONG
COMMEMORATIVE
BRICKS.

BILLY PAYNE WAS OVERCOME BY EMOTION AS HE TALKED TO GEORGIA GOV. ZELL MILLER AND **ACOG** CHIEF OPERATING OFFICER A.D. FRAZIER AT MEMORIAL SERVICE IN THE PARK.

BILL CRANFORD

A RALLYING CRY TO CONTINUE: TENS OF THOUSANDS JAMMED CENTENNIAL PARK FOR A MEMORIAL SERVICE FOR THE BOMBING VICTIMS.

THE NAYSAYERS WERE
WRONG. THE PEOPLE
RETURNED TO THE PARK,
AND IN LARGER NUMBERS
THAN EVER. A THURSDAY
NIGHT CONCERT BY
RAY CHARLES WAS
WALL-TO-WALL HUMANITY.

CHAPTER 8

A Job Well Done

A FINAL FIREWORKS DISPLAY, THEN IT WAS TIME TO TURN
OUT THE LIGHTS — AND THE OLYMPIC FLAME — ON THE
GREATEST SPECTACLE ATLANTA HAD EVER SEEN.

RENEE HANNANS

JOHN SPINK

ONE GLORIOUS SUMMER

8 A JOB WELL DONE

The End of an Incredible Journey

I T HAPPENED SO QUICKLY. ONE FINAL SHOW. POWERFUL SINGING, DANCING, SOME skateboarders, a couple of speeches, one last parade of athletes, some fireworks.

Then ... poof.

It was over.

One minute, Atlanta was at the center of the universe, hosting world leaders, the greatest athletes on the planet, more celebrities than L.A., and visitors from every land. For a few weeks one special summer, downtown rocked 24-hours a day, people danced in the streets, traded pins and wore silly hats. Strangers smiled and exchanged greetings.

Then, in the blink of an eye, t-shirts were two for $10.

Anybody get the number of that truck?

The end of an incredible journey.

For six years, Atlanta prepared — dreaming, scheming, sweating, paving, planting, building, demolishing and polishing — for 17 sweet days in the spotlight. Then, before it seemed the paint was fully dry, the world was gone.

Atlanta's big show closed memorably as Gloria Estefan, Stevie Wonder (left), B.B. King and Little Richard entertained one last full house at the Olympic

FRANK NIEMEIR

stadium. A world TV audience, estimated at more than a billion, watched the caldron flame flicker out, and heard the call to reconvene four years hence, in Sydney, Australia.

Left in the wake, along with all the cleaning up and breaking down, expressions of gratitude from many satisfied visitors, impressed most by Atlanta's greatest resource, the hospitality of its people.

Certainly, considering the years Atlanta had to ponder the arrival of the Olympics, it will spend many more years in reflection.

And those memories, most assuredly, will be warm and comforting, resting in the knowledge of a job well done — and One Glorious Summer.

ONE GLORIOUS SUMMER

THE FLAGS OF 197 NATIONS ROLLED INTO OLYMPIC STADIUM
ONE LAST TIME, AS DID ACROBATIC SKATEBOARDERS AND
MOUNTAIN BIKERS IN A HIGH-ENERGY CLOSING.

ANDY SHARP

DAVE CRUZ

IN THE AFTERMATH,
ATLANTANS WERE LEFT WITH
A MASSIVE CLEAN UP,
WHILE VISITORS RUSHED
FOR THE EXITS — AND
THE AIRPORT.

ONE GLORIOUS SUMMER

JEAN SHIFRIN

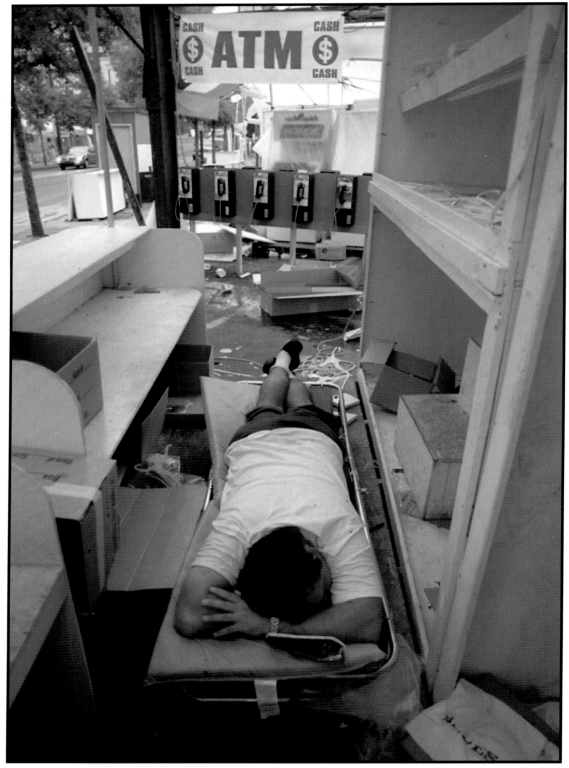

ANDY SHARP

THE DAY AFTER. THE PEOPLE HAVE GONE, THE SHELVES ARE EMPTY.
GREAT TIME TO REST — IT'S ONLY FOUR YEARS 'TIL SYDNEY.